I Am
Losing Signal!

I Am
Losing Signal!

Connecting with our 'Real' self

Ritendra Banerjee

author HOUSE®

AuthorHouse™
1663 Liberty Drive
Bloomington, IN 47403
www.authorhouse.com
Phone: 1-800-839-8640

Published by AuthorHouse   05/07/2013

ISBN: 978-1-4817-4332-7 (sc)
ISBN: 978-1-4817-4331-0 (hc)
ISBN: 978-1-4817-4330-3 (e)

Library of Congress Control Number: 2013908343

For, Of, By

My parents for giving me life
All my life coaches for enriching it

Inspirations

Swami Sukhabodhananda ji*
Robin Sharma (www.robinsharma.com)

*For Swamiji's tailor-made corporate interventions and seminars, contact

+9199017 77006, +91-80-4153 5834.
www.prasannatrust.org

I hope to wake up with a dream about You and me forever . . . even when sleeping with a reality without You now?

Preface

Experience is a great teacher, but the emphasis is rarely on the student.

I wonder what a great teacher would do in an empty classroom with no student!

I feel like a student now.

I am, perhaps, going through one of the most defining of "life experiences" as I write this.

Interestingly, in my notebook's folder is a business book project that I started a few years ago. Yes, a few years ago.

This was a natural progression, given my background in business and my having had the good fortune of coauthoring two books before.

But I am currently more motivated to address and manifest life issues first. Business can wait!

In a world full of mobile phones and computers, a wise man once said, "In spite of being so well-connected [technologically speaking], we are still so little connected [person to person]."

As I look around and reflect on life connections, a very common saying and imagery comes across: "I am losing signal!"

Perhaps there are similarities between "losing signal" and life.

A good starting point may be to list the places where we normally lose signal.

The elevator. Perhaps this is a reflection of the lack of human connection, as there is only so much space inside an elevator. Didn't someone once say relationships are also about space?

I wonder where else we could be losing signal. If frogs could use mobile handsets, and they jumped into a well, perhaps there is only so much signal one can get in the frog's world, which is so very restricted inside the well. Talk of a frog in the well!

Crowded marketplaces may have too much noise and clutter for people to even realize that someone is speaking, and this may be mistaken as just because one can't hear (and listen) that there is no signal.

The following pages are a reflection of my discovery as I go through life.

In the first part of the book, I use the imagery of calls and signals, reflecting on some key cornerstones of my life. In the second part, I share what am aspiring to practice: to make all sixty seconds in a minute count. I must confess I am far from it. I have structured these practices as questions that you may use to call into life's "call center,"

And finally an ode.

You can read the book in any way and reflect similarly.

I may not be wise enough to prescribe, but I am experienced enough to describe.

As my friend said yesterday, "He who needs to learn the most probably has most to share." Happy reading!

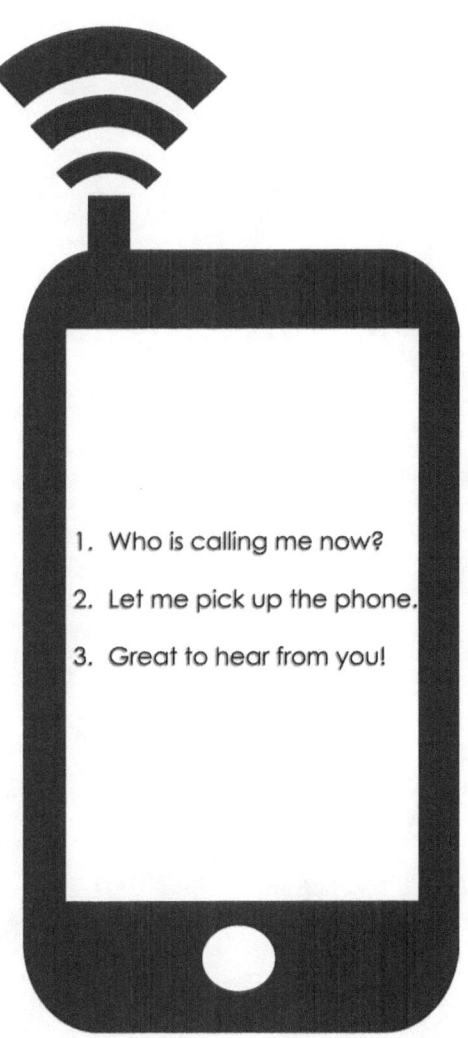

1. Who is calling me now?

2. Let me pick up the phone.

3. Great to hear from you!

1. Who is calling me now?

This question reminds me of a popular book and movie in which God was calling.

Our daily phone call logs show that people know us and call us. Some people may not know us but have our records (the quintessential telemarketer) and call us as well. Then we have the wrong connections.

Something that strikes me is that many times, we are more polite responding to wrong connections than to people we know.

I wonder why.

Is it that we have a definitive mental model of who the people we know are?

Is it that we believe every telemarketer is out to sell? Because I patiently listen to some of them, by chance I realize that many of them are calling me for feedback to make their services better or perhaps to give me a gift that I deserve.

Perhaps someone is reaching out for me to contribute to his or her well-being and growth?

Then there are people who call us to give us good news. Bad news. Useless news. Useful news. Is it fair to assume that, just because a friend is calling, it will always be good news or to assume that, if a competitor is calling, it will always be bad news?

Why do we prejudge?

As Buddha once said, "A person cannot take bath in the same river twice, because the river has flowed."

Why do we assume that every situation with a person is going to be similar?

On a related note, perhaps the best love stories are those that have variety. It is not about spicing life up. It is about being free and open to life, not having prejudgments.

The more we put into life, the more it gives us.

The challenge is this: how do we grow in spite of ourselves?

2. Let me pick up the phone.

Have you ever been to a game arcade and watched your kids shooting at targets?

Most often, the best scores happen not when they fire and then aim nor when they aim and then fire, but when they do a little of both.

Answering calls is a bit like that. Responding to a call for a relationship is a bit like that.

I wonder if one can ever plan to initiate and be in a relationship, unless we are talking of matrimony or dating sites. (I wonder which ones last longer these days!)

Somewhere out there our sense of picking up the phone reflects how we embark on relationships, how we see our past, our current "state of being," and maybe how we long for the future (say, if that phone call is from the head of HR, who may be calling to offer that big package).

As we pick up the call, we may be modeled by who we are and what we have been through. Some people pick up the call "just like that," whereas some are meticulous about checking to see whether it is someone they know and decide whether to pick up or not pick up (response).

As I look at the call timers on my phone, I realize that I have received four times more calls than I have made. (And here I thought I was a consultant who sold for a living!) I recall doing a similar stock take five years back. The statistics were just the opposite.

As I reflect, I realize that maybe I am at a stage of life where I am not embarking on new relationships as much as being grateful to God for the ones I have and nurturing them—maybe spending more time with these relationships, some of whom may actually cry when I die. Maybe I am being able to let people "in."

3. Great to hear from you!

"Hey, thanks for calling."

"Long time, no see."

"Would you mind not disturbing me now?"

"Go to hell. I don't want to talk to you."

We may be using the same set of ears that God has given us, the same phone, but what comes through could be so very different.

Wouldn't it be easier to believe that, irrespective of the call script, it is great to hear from the other person?

Through what that person is conveying may be a life lesson, an opportunity to give in the truest sense.

Perhaps "Would you mind not disturbing me now?" could help us be more patient. The sacred texts talk about *titiksha* (forbearance) as a key cornerstone of life. As I write this, I am patiently waiting to relive in a more positive way a relationship that I hold in the dearest sense, but one that I had a huge role in messing up.

"Go to hell. I don't want to talk to you" could mean that I will talk to you when you to go to heaven. I once read, "If you treat me like a queen, I will treat you like a king." That's simple, isn't it?

A qualifier: it is better not to expect to be treated like a king or even to be the king.

If the cosmic forces have enough positive energy that one has been able to create by treating the other person as a queen, it will happen anyway.

The queen-king analogy can be extended to a two friends ("if you treat me like a friend, the positive energy and forces will cause me to treat you so as well), boss-subordinate (respect is mutually earned, not demanded) and so on.

Wasn't it a wise scientist who once observed, "e=mc²," that is, energy and mass are interchangeable and morphable. When we die and are buried or cremated, don't we all turn into mass and energy as well? (Have you ever observed the flakes emanating out of the pyre?) Why is it that it takes a death experience to understand what is actually a life experience?

Notes:

_____

_____

_____

_____

_____

_____

_____

_____

_____

_____

_____

_____

_____

_____

_____

_____

_____

_____

_____

_____

_____

_____

_____

_____

Notes:

_____

_____

_____

_____

_____

_____

_____

_____

_____

_____

_____

_____

_____

_____

_____

_____

_____

_____

_____

_____

_____

_____

_____

_____

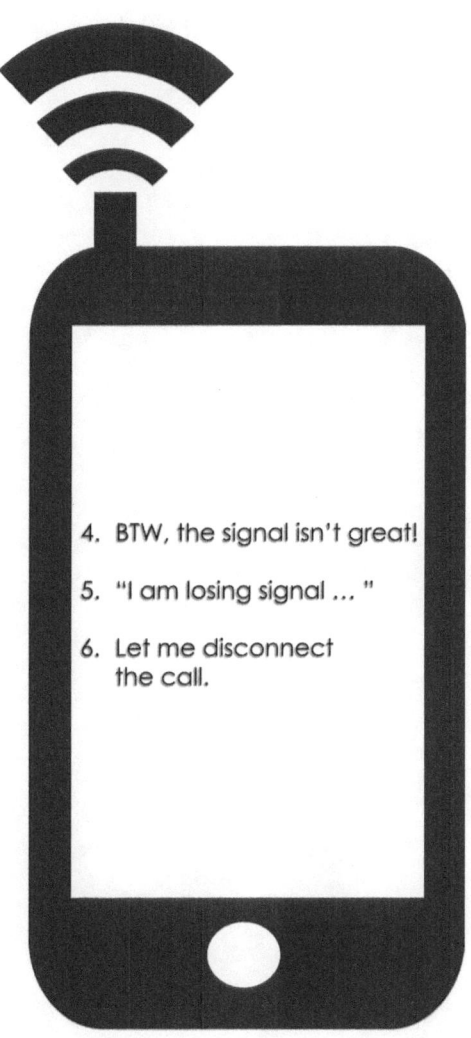

4. BTW, the signal isn't great!

5. "I am losing signal … "

6. Let me disconnect
   the call.

4. BTW, the signal isn't great!

Rather than disconnect and dial or message back, we continue to talk.

We hope the signal gets better so we can hear each other.

We continue to battle the forces of nature and bandwidth, thinking the signal (connection) will improve.

When was the last time we reflected on the best way to deal with life's waves?

Is it by fighting the waves or floating with them?

As one in among a billion subscribers, we may not have the luxury of influencing mobile networks.

But being one among billions of planets, we do have the luxury of influencing our life's networks.

Who we are is in our hands, and that truly determines what is on our hands. Medical science has proven that, even late in life, palm lines do change, influenced by physiological factors and our "state of being."

I would not even attempt to guess what the palm lines of the greats were.

I would certainly be excited to draw inspiration from what they did, what was in their hands, because they chose to let their palms open up, to allow their palms to grip life's situations with all their might, humility, strength, and wisdom.

Can we just open up our palms right now, close our eyes, and prepare to grip what we must to live life fully and well?

The saddest situation in life is when "die today" but are "buried after a decade"—or maybe a couple of them.

5. "I am losing signal ..."

Have you ever wondered when one gets more irritated: when one loses signal right at the beginning of a call or when one is in the middle of a conversation?

Chances are it is the latter.

Relationships are probably a lot like that.

Most frustrations and anger and everything irritating happens when one is deeply in the middle of it all and suddenly begins to lose the signal.

However, my experience shows that, if the intent is for a true, lifelong connection, a deep-rooted one at that, the signal will be restored, just like that! Magic!

The connection will stay in spite of a temporary loss of signal.

All it takes is a smile, a hug, a confession, being accountable and responsible, true commitment.

As I write this, I am in the middle of a signal-restoration project.

I can tell you this: all it takes is the look in the other person's eye to know what this relationship really means and doesn't mean.

A good friend of mine, who heads strategy for a telecommunications company, tells me that even networks have an intuitive ability, given all things equal, not to drop a call with a frequent caller! Technology mirrors life, doesn't it?

After all, software is nothing but a programmable extension of the human mind.

I wish we could also be like software, programming and programmed for all the good and nice things in life.

6. Let me disconnect the call.

It takes a certain ability to appreciate that even good signals mean nothing if the person at the other end is keen to disconnect my call(s).

Perhaps there isn't a real connection.

I have been reflecting on the number of times that I have knowingly disconnected calls.

It gives me some amount of pride to say, "Rarely."

And it is not that I pick up all calls.

Some I don't pick up; I let the call be.

Many times, when I have been disconnected, I was left with some amount of rejection.

It is this experience that makes me wonder if letting calls be, rather than disconnecting, gives people a little more peace in thinking that I may have missed the call and will call back.

A voice mail or perhaps a quick SMS could help acknowledge that one will reach the other person.

When I have messaged back to unknown numbers to check on who it is and say that I will call back if required, I have had the pleasant joys of not missing out on valuable opportunities to make a difference to others' lives. I have experienced this many a time with child-help organizations' help lines' chasing me, among others.

All I am trying to share is that maybe there is merit in not disconnecting life's calls and letting calls be.

Notes:

_____

_____

_____

_____

_____

_____

_____

_____

_____

_____

_____

_____

_____

_____

_____

_____

_____

_____

_____

_____

_____

_____

_____

_____

Notes:

_____

_____

_____

_____

_____

_____

_____

_____

_____

_____

_____

_____

_____

_____

_____

_____

_____

_____

_____

_____

_____

_____

_____

_____

_____

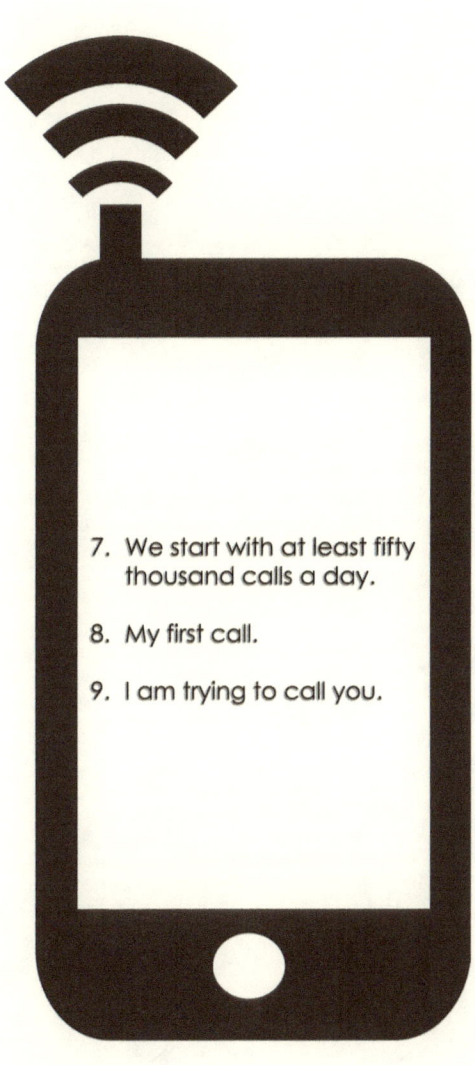

7. We start with at least fifty thousand calls a day.

8. My first call.

9. I am trying to call you.

7. We start with at least fifty thousand calls a day.

Even if we haven't called anyone in a day—try doing it; it is so peaceful to be alone for twenty-four hours, although I am saying "alone" and not "lonely"—we still have more than fifty thousand calls to deal with.

This is the number of calls that we are making inside us. This is the number of thoughts that typically go through our minds every day.

It is a paradox that the best call quality when we are speaking with someone is not determined so much by what is happening outside—the handset, networks and so on—but what is happening inside: inside the caller and inside the receiver, the called.

Research shows that most of these calls—as much as 85 percent of them—are related to the past.

About 10 percent are related to the future.

Only 5 percent are related to here and now.

And it is the here and now on which we have most influence.

What a pity that we are not making more here-and-now calls and "living in the moment."

What is most in our control is something we least try to control; we cannot change the past and we can create a future only by fully living and working in the present. The "present" is truly a "gift."

Some of these inner calls are good thoughts: "I will help a poor child today."

Some are bad: "Let me mess up his happiness."

Some are useless: "I am wondering what he or she is thinking now." (You can't control what he or she is thinking now, so why break your head?)

Some are necessary: "I need to go to the station today."

With uncontrolled minds, which most of us live and "swear" by (literally), we tend to bundle a good or even useless thought with a bad one, so "I need to go to the station today" is normally followed by "and what a mess the traffic and this city are!"

Our natural tendency is to seek solace in the bad (to generate lots of sympathy) when we live in a world that gives a lot of good, even for good feelings, even when we haven't done something good.

On second thought, you have actually done something good when you have good feelings. By feeling good, you have released all the positive and "feel-good" hormones inside your body. You have added to your breath and, through that, a little more to your life.

That's a start!

8. My first call.

The first call I made on my first mobile phone was to my mother. When I ask friends, most of them remember who got their first mobile phone call. Of course, there are a few who do end up with, "The salesman who sold my SIM to me; I wanted to ensure it worked!"

For the record, it doesn't matter who it was.

What does matter is the excitement of the first call before the second call happened and the third . . . and so on until the excitement of calling died down or perhaps we got another new mobile, a better version. And so on.

- When did I first learn to walk? Or did I learn? Nah, when did I first walk?
- When did I first talk?
- When did I first fall off a bicycle?
- When did I first lose my cool?
- When did I first break a bone?
- When did I first break someone else's bone (if that has ever happened)?
- When did I first eat pizza?
- When did I first cut classes?

We usually remember most of these "firsts" if they're positive moments but rarely the "firsts" that are negative moments unless the magnitude of those negative moments was so huge that we can never ever forget. Some of these negative "firsts" are etched in my heart and even amnesia may not erase them from my mind unless I train my mind to do so! This is one the many bases for taking to meditate.

9. I am trying to call you.

Many times we try to call another person and can't reach him or her.

I have noticed that, typically, the calls that don't go through (barring network problems) are the ones I made when I was trying to connect with the other person "just like that," or maybe with not enough positive intent. I was trying to connect "with the person" rather than connecting "out of myself" with him or her.

In simple terms, what it means is the power of making calls with no agenda.

When we speak with near and dear ones, don't we normally connect out of ourselves with no-agenda calls, unless life's necessities require us to discuss an agenda like a business proposition or the latest movies to hit town. The operative words here are "intent" and "warmth."

Another context of "I am trying to call you" could also be when you need help.

There have been times when I have called someone to seek some help, or advice when really what I was looking for was some time and warmth. The other person was busy and I felt more messed up after calling than I was before, reflecting on why did I not get someone to share with.

Is there really a right time to call?

Is there really a right place to call from?

Isn't there more to life than planning?

Isn't life about living in the moment?

Notes:

_____

_____

_____

_____

_____

_____

_____

_____

_____

_____

_____

_____

_____

_____

_____

_____

_____

_____

_____

_____

_____

_____

_____

_____

_____

_____

_____

Notes:

_____

_____

_____

_____

_____

_____

_____

_____

_____

_____

_____

_____

_____

_____

_____

_____

_____

_____

_____

_____

_____

_____

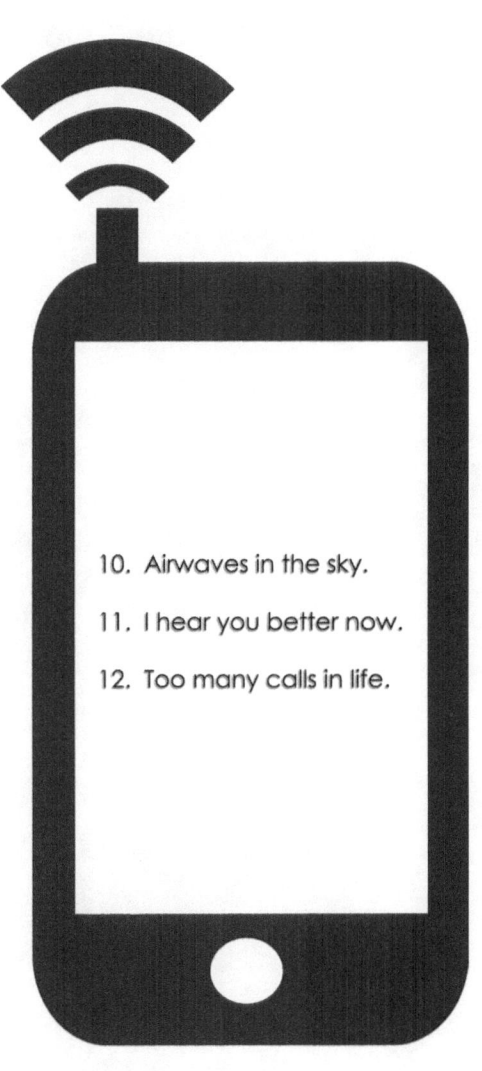

10. Airwaves in the sky.

11. I hear you better now.

12. Too many calls in life.

10. Airwaves in the sky.

The drive to my office takes me through the lanes of the city until I hit the expressway.

I like—no, I love—watching the sky.

The clouds stay. Some move. The hue of the sky changes. The sun eases a bit through the clouds at times.

It is so beautiful.

My mind wanders, and I start wondering whether I could be like the airwaves, airwaves that provide a basis for people to connect, that could provide a medium for nature to connect.

As I reflect more deeply, I wonder whether airwaves also end up interfering with people and other beings.

A bad airwave could scare a bird away.

A bad airwave could drop that important call.

And more . . .

Maybe there is more basis in being the Sky, rather than wanting to be like it. Maybe that's a formula not to want anything.

Overencompassing.

Infinite.

Natural.

Letting people be.

Letting the birds fly.

Letting the clouds meander.

Letting the airplane take a mother home.

Letting myself be around for those lovely fireworks at the Hong Kong Harbor. Or the Diwali night, back in India.

Giving indications to people about whether it will be a sunny day or it will rain.

Being the happy sky with all the sunshine.

Being the cloudy sky with all the heaviness of the heart.

And at times letting oneself be. To cry. To rain.

The relief and the expressions that come with it.

My rain helps crops prosper.

Gets that little girl to dance out of happiness, rather than dancing for happiness.

Why not?

And then I realize that airwaves are best held in the sky.

What would airwaves be anyway without the sky?

11. I hear you better now.

If I can never be the person I wish to be, I will always be the person I could never become. Chill! It's just a frame of reference for us to see ourselves.

Such a frame is a paradigm, the way we see the world.

Many times I wonder why, in spite of a bad call connection, I still hear the other person so clearly.

Does it boil down to my state of being at the time of the call? Maybe I have just finished a lovely lunch and have all the gumption I need to do justice to that call?

Or is there something deeper? I imagine that most of it has to do with our paradigms.

This reminds me of the classic story in which a young office-goer becomes irritated by the noise a few kids are making in a train station. It is early morning and all is quiet; one expected it to be quiet day all day.

This irritated man walks up to the father of the kids and says, "Why the hell don't you stop them?"

The father apologizes and says, "I am sorry. These kids have just lost their mother,"

The office-goer's paradigm shifts, and he regrets having expressed himself as he did.

Many times in life we understand others better because we understand our paradigms better.

Understanding one's own paradigm starts with understanding oneself. It also starts with understanding the other by listening, not just hearing.

Listening requires true empathy, which is not putting oneself into the other person's shoes, but first taking one's own shoes off, and then putting oneself into the other's shoes.

I am learning the hard way.

12. Too many calls in life.

The power of S-I-L-E-N-C-E.

Spirituality

Inside

Listened

Enhanced

Nurtured

Contemplated

Executed

In simple words, silence soothes. Part of the reason is that we are burning less energy, unless we aspire to burn more in a truly meditative way.

Silence gets better if we close our eyes, as that helps in repressing further energy loss.

We have the biggest family disputes in all the silent, posh colonies of big cities because there is silence outside, but not inside.

When was the last time you closed your eyes and experienced your breath?

When was the last time you felt silence within yourself?

The other day, a close friend of mine called me and inquired as to what is the best way to start meditating.

The experience I shared was, for starters, not to try to meditate but simply to sit with legs crossed and eyes closed for as long as possible and, if possible, experience one's breath. This practice is usually called Zazen.

That is a start because that will quiet the restlessness that comes from our life clutter. Afterward, it will give rise to a phase of becoming creatively restless.

One could move to more formal forms of meditation. A string in any internet search engine will show us approaches and techniques.

Like the cookie advertisement, I dare say that any time and any place is a good time and place for meditation.

I have even practiced meditation while waiting for eggs to boil in the kettle!

Whenever you feel like meditating, feel free (literally).

(Let us also remember that a fool with a technique is still a fool!)

Notes:

_____

_____

_____

_____

_____

_____

_____

_____

_____

_____

_____

_____

_____

_____

_____

_____

_____

_____

_____

_____

_____

_____

_____

Notes:

_____

_____

_____

_____

_____

_____

_____

_____

_____

_____

_____

_____

_____

_____

_____

_____

_____

_____

_____

_____

_____

_____

_____

_____

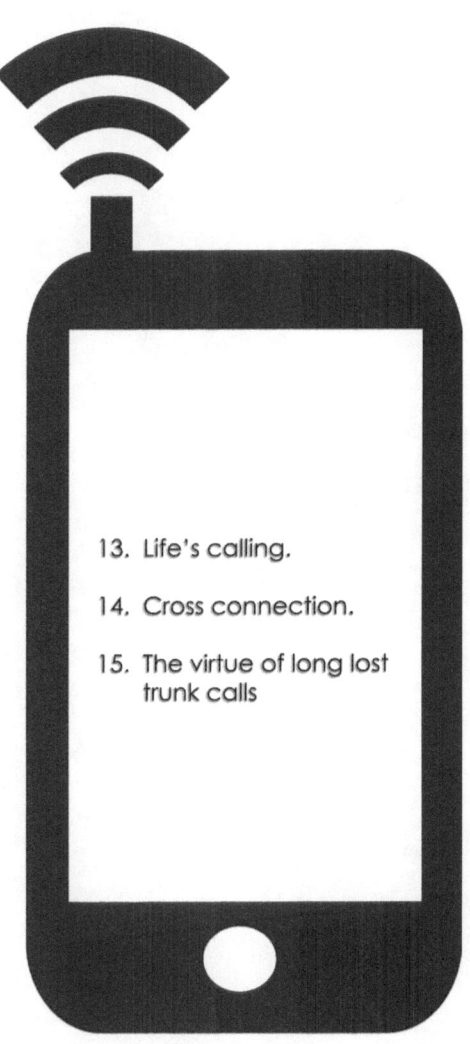

13. Life's calling

What we like in life (and in business) may not be what we get. What we want, we may get. What we truly and deeply aspire to we will surely achieve.

I am saying this based on my experience.

I practiced this so well at work. I wonder why. Does it come with a certain relative sense of detachment vis-à-vis life, to which we are so attached?

The irony is that maybe life needs us to be more aware of our ability to detach, as the stakes are high. Really high.

A friend of mine who is very successful in life and business practices what he calls "detached attachment." Developing an appetite to truly experience (to the point of savoring) people, places and things that are important, but having the wisdom not to get glued to them, so that it does not hurt if experiences from these did not match to what one was looking for. To that extent, staying detached as well.

By the time I realized this deep reality, I initially felt it was too late.

I continue to truly and deeply aspire now . . . .

Maybe this is an experience that is normally what one calls life's calling: to be, to give everything to that one thing or person that matters the most.

No one can take that away.

If I could capture this moment, it would be like *The Lion King's* Simba standing on top of the rock, reflecting on what was to be and not to be, and soaking in the vastness that lay before him.

Perhaps we meet people for a reason.

I met a person who changed so much in me, and only when I knew I was truly conscious of all the good changes that I was striving to make came God's calling and that person moved on.

Maybe this person is a true life coach. Some people may call it soul mate.

I am not romanticizing these notions; I truly believe in them for the simple reason that sometimes we feel the blessing and vibration of someone else much better when we are apart than when we are close. We feel it inside.

This is the gift I had the privilege of receiving.

This person continues to inspire me to do whatever little good I can in this beautiful world.

I feel inspired to live with this person inside me and manifest that power in giving and being good.

When we hold pain in front of a mirror, it reflects, and through that reflection emerges an inverse image, that of pleasure and goodness.

I feel like a butterfly, light and colorful.

I feel like an eagle, soaring and focused.

I feel like a cheetah, aware of and alert to the immense possibilities of life through my life's calling.

When was the last time life called you? When was the last time you allowed life to call you, opened yourself out, to let life in?

14. Cross connection.

Cross connections can be chaotic.

All the parties are trying to speak with each other, maybe with a lot of good intent, but, alas!

When the cross connections persist (and, yes, I am talking about people talking back at each other in anger and sadness as well), it can really hurt!

There is a life and spiritual concept called the Tango Theory. As people, we all have wounds inside us. When we are too close to someone in life, dancing life like a tango, we may end up aligning our wounds unknowingly and rubbing them against each other.

Our intent may not be to do so, but it could occur with some close cross connections.

On wiser reflection on life, am not sure whether we can always avoid rubbing these wounds together.

However, what we can be aware of is the need to be kind to each other. I reiterate that it may not always matter whether we are right or wrong in life. What does matter is whether we are kind.

15. The virtue of long lost trunk calls.

I remember days when one of the most eagerly awaited moments of our lives was the call-back ring of a trunk call.

I remember my parents' booking these calls, and then the telephone folks would connect with the target number and call us back.

Patience was key, as many times the call back would happen only after hours had passed.

Patient we were. For a phone call helped us connect with someone we wanted to speak to, having not heard each other for a while.

Those were the days of postcards and letters that brought magic to our lives in writing and reading those letters. Those were also the days of the Telex.

Those were the days before mobile phones and emails took over and aligned our call connections (and maybe our relationships as well) so we were instantly gratified to the extent that we lost our cool if we did not get signal immediately. I was guilty of that many times, but not now as I write this book in near wilderness, having switched off my phone.

The virtue of long-lost trunk calls shows us what simple pleasures in life meant.

I am not taking away from what my professor in business school once said, that "every generation has to shed its own tears."

I do appreciate the upsides of modern technology.

The challenge is whether we can stay on top of it and live our lives with the conviction of being truly connected.

It doesn't matter if there is signal on my mobile phone *now*.

Notes:

_____

_____

_____

_____

_____

_____

_____

_____

_____

_____

_____

_____

_____

_____

_____

_____

_____

_____

_____

_____

_____

_____

_____

_____

_____

Notes:

_____

_____

_____

_____

_____

_____

_____

_____

_____

_____

_____

_____

_____

_____

_____

_____

_____

_____

_____

_____

_____

_____

_____

_____

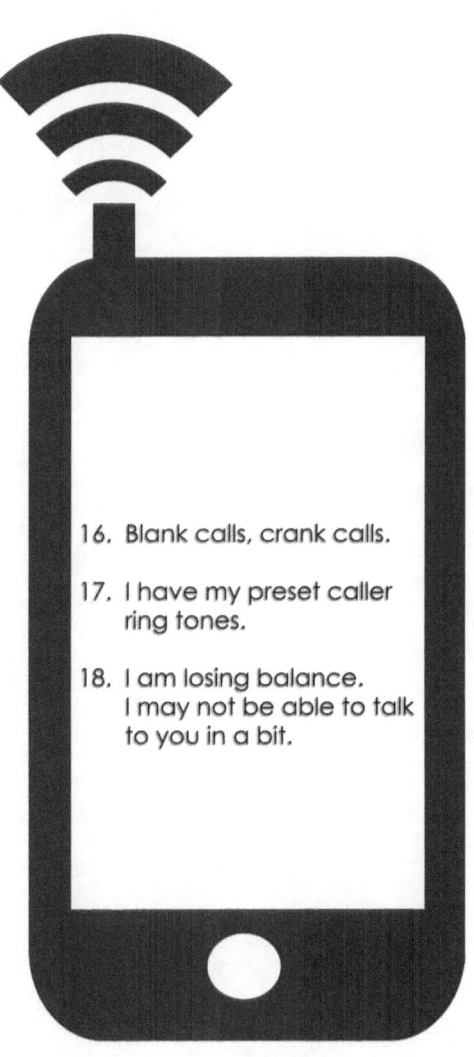

16. Blank calls, crank calls.

17. I have my preset caller ring tones.

18. I am losing balance. I may not be able to talk to you in a bit.

16. Blank calls, crank calls.

Some of the best love stories started with blank calls and crank calls.

Some of the worst conspiracies were also launched through these methods.

The point I am trying to reiterate is that there is power in silence—or, rather, S-I-L-E-N-C-E.

Someone I am very close to taught me this.

Many times, when we wanted to say something, we messaged each other with a blank SMS.

The message came with the messenger.

I was and continue to be the talkative kind. That is the way I am wired.

However, having been through the heat and grime of relationships, I am beginning to appreciate the power of being quiet. Of being calm. Of being calmly active. Of being actively calm.

I am striving to get to the point when I get to practice this with everyone, and consciously at that. I will always be thankful for the lovely gift that this person has left me.

God bless you!

17. I have my preset caller ring tones.

I have my preset caller ring tones, so I know who is calling.

Great!

But what do I know beyond the preset caller ring tone, as in, the person?

I am assuming that this effort of knowing the person is worth it, at least for people who are in our inner circles.

I tried reflecting on this with some of my closest relationships, and this is what I found:

	What I know about this person	What I don't know about this person
I know	This may seem easy, but it is not. Most expectation mismatches happen because we assume what we know. I am trying to use life's toughest situations as a backdrop to understanding people because that is when their true selves are revealed.	Try asking! If the person is close enough and open to sharing, I will know. That will also help me understand the phase of the relationship I am in with that person, including his or her comfort level.

I don't know	Try looking for other good qualities beyond what I know. By doing this, I will get to see a bit more of the nice person that this person is. I will also be more inspired.	Let it be. Life will show up. We may have no-shows in flights and movie theatres, but never in life. Nature is slow to let us know her secrets, but she does not tell lies.

18. I am losing balance. I may not be able to talk to you in a bit.

How true the threat of not being able to continue talking for all prepaid mobile customers when it comes to calling.

How true for all people when it comes to life.

As I reflect on the moments when I lost balance, I recall imagining I was in one of life's tough situations when I did the following:

- Called someone I wanted to talk to and got no response
- Wanted a hug, said it, but didn't get it
- Wasn't strong enough to write it down (e-mails included)
- Didn't talk to myself

I realize more and more that inner balance brings in outer balance.

If I am the "ruler of my soul and the master of my destiny," is it fair that I ever lose balance?

Human beings are not just marvels of engineering. We also have a management side to our beings, which is what makes each one of us unique.

Two hundred and six bones and 10 to the power of 13 neurons is what all normal human beings are bestowed with. That is nature's engineering.

What we do with these bones and brains is left to each one of us. That is the "management" bit in us.

It is only natural that we lose balance at times. That is okay. It is okay to cry! Real men and women cry.

What matters is not whether we lose balance but whether we use that experience to create a better balance, a better equilibrium.

Balance is ensuring that the left and right sides of a scale are at the same level: something like joy = sorrow.

Equilibrium is like using the best machine to weigh. It doesn't matter if joy is not equal to sorrow, but is their equilibrium making me a better person? Is it making me more resolute? Is it letting me open up and experience life in ways I have never experienced it before? Is it propelling my hormones and neurotransmitters to make me calmer and more alert and focused as a person?

People with equilibrium are usually also the people who get a very good night's sleep, irrespective of the hours they sleep.

Notes:

_____

_____

_____

_____

_____

_____

_____

_____

_____

_____

_____

_____

_____

_____

_____

_____

_____

_____

_____

_____

_____

_____

_____

_____

_____

_____

_____

_____

Notes:

_____

_____

_____

_____

_____

_____

_____

_____

_____

_____

_____

_____

_____

_____

_____

_____

_____

_____

_____

_____

_____

_____

_____

_____

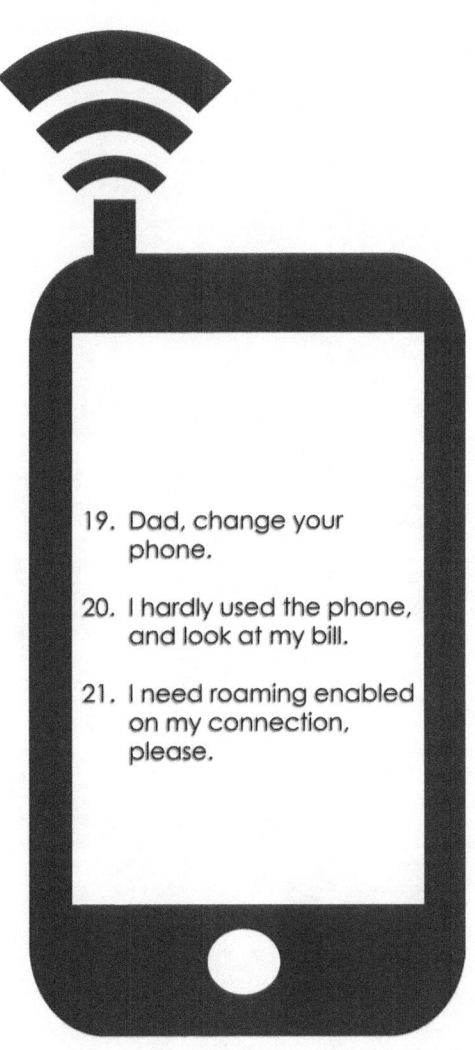

19. Dad, change your phone.

20. I hardly used the phone, and look at my bill.

21. I need roaming enabled on my connection, please.

19. Dad, change your phone.

I continued to encourage dad till recently, that he changes his phone so he can hear better, but he refused.

And as I reflect on this problem, I realize something very basic: most places where our fancy phones may not have worked, Dad's phone did!

It may be battered. It may be old. But it is robust.

At the risk of stretching the point, the more I see Dad's phone, the more am reminded of what Kahlil Girbran once said: "Out of suffering emerge the strongest souls. The most massive characters are seared with the most scars."

Whether it is old being gold or that car of mine that I never imagine I will sell because it is so much a part of me and I am so much a part of it or that old pair of jeans that still fits, I wonder whether it is merely for sentimental reasons that we don't let go of such things. (I know someone who even refuses to let go of his old underwear.)

I really don't think so. If we can let go of people, surely we can let go of these other things.

However, what I am beginning to be convinced of is that maybe it has to do with these things having gone through life with me, through thick and thin.

It's the company we have kept, whether a nonliving being or a living being, the watch that I never wear but won't give away its "tick" and "tock."

20. I hardly used the phone, and look at my bill.

It happens to us all the time.

It takes a bill to realize that we have spoken so much.

Sometimes in life it doesn't matter how much more or less, we speak.

All the matters is what we said. Or didn't say. That one moment of fury. That one flash of anger. That outburst that was not meant for the person who was in front of me but for someone else.

The deepest relationships are founded on silence, and the ones that got lost in that silence were the ones with the most "noise."

So what's our bill for life? What are we destined to pay? What do we bring upon us as additional payments over and above what we are destined to pay anyway?

I believe that life also comes with its cover charges or, in the language of calls, subscription charges. But these are not the ones that pinch.

The ones that pinch and hurt are the ones that we have brought upon ourselves.

We can never buy these; we bring them ourselves.

We can never buy relationships; we can only bring (in) relationships, like that home run that won the game while someone close was watching and feeling proud.

Like that oatmeal cookie that was served with so much love, and it didn't matter where the cookie came from as much as what it meant.

We have to pay our bills, and sometimes we pay much more than we thought we needed to.

But then God and the human spirit shows us how we can afford to pay these bills and grow wiser—maybe move to a smarter subscription plan as well. Those things that motivate us to be "life subscribers" for true bliss are love, respect, kindness, and compassion.

21. I need roaming enabled on my connection, please.

It happens to us all the time.

We go to a new city, village, or country and we realize we aren't connected.

However, here is the good news: Life is full on with roaming. We don't have to enable it. Nature has done the job. All we have to do is activate our instruments, our senses, our beliefs, our paradigms.

It is the same set of values and feelings that connect us with others, irrespective of where we are.

Love gets love.

Honesty gets honesty.

A mother in Honolulu has the same feelings for her child as a mother in Bathinda.

A lover in the Alps has the same "dhak dhak" (heart beat) happening as Munna and Banno in a Taru village (back in the hinterlands of India).

The boundaries around which we manage ourselves (remember: management of the human being) are pretty much the same everywhere. The realities and the degrees may vary.

Why would this life roaming not be possible? After all, each human being on this planet is separated from even the most distant other human being by only six degrees of relationship.

Amazing, isn't it?

I am currently trying to figure out my connections to some powerful world leaders!

PS: When was the last time you thought you needed a Visa for love or friendship?

Notes:

_____

_____

_____

_____

_____

_____

_____

_____

_____

_____

_____

_____

_____

_____

_____

_____

_____

_____

_____

_____

_____

_____

_____

_____

Notes:

_____

_____

_____

_____

_____

_____

_____

_____

_____

_____

_____

_____

_____

_____

_____

_____

_____

_____

_____

_____

_____

_____

_____

_____

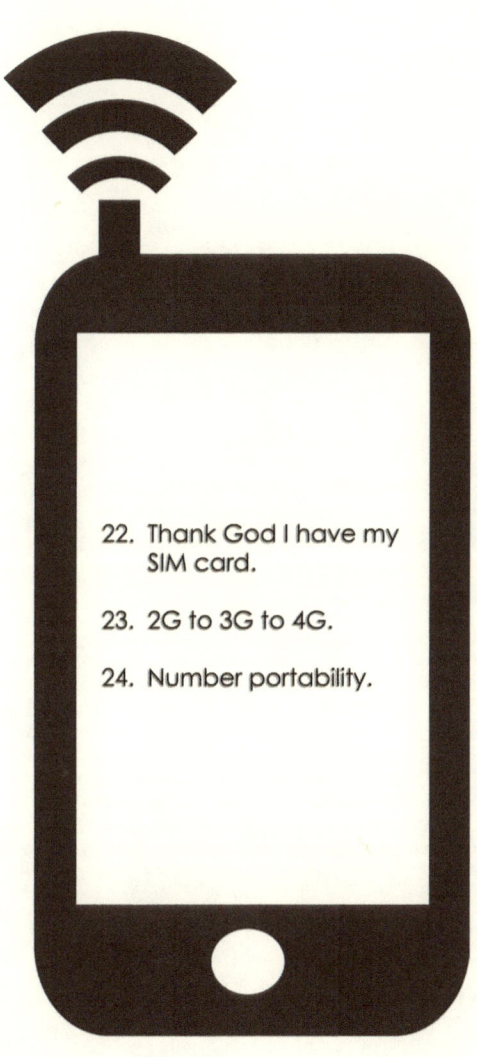

22. Thank God I have my SIM card.

23. 2G to 3G to 4G.

24. Number portability.

22. Thank God I have my SIM card.

A SIM is like our values. It stays with us.

It doesn't matter where we are, in what context, using which phone (our emotions).

It stays.

SIM also stores all our contacts and relationships and aggregates them in terms of who we are and what drives us.

It is the heart of who we are.

It doesn't matter which of our relationships are active or who our favorite callers are.

For a SIM, it is all the same.

Values democratize us.

They don't drive us to apply a little more value to one person and less to someone else.

They help us treat everyone with the same courtesy and respect.

Relationships can be made or broken depending on the quality of one's SIMs.

The unfortunate reality is that sometimes other people mistake our state of being as wrong values.

Only if that person takes a deeper look at the person who also brings in glimpses of joy can he or she see the real you. And maybe all that is needed is to string those glimpses of joy into a life picture that is happy and nice.

While emotional attunement is important, value attunement is critical.

23. 2G to 3G to 4G.

We have had our share of news on these 2G, 3G, and 4G mobile telephony networks.

In some ways, I believe our life journeys are about moving from one spectrum to another.

2G:

- Being **G**ood
- Showing **G**oodness

3G:

- Being **G**ood
- Showing **G**oodness
- Feeling **G**reat

4G:

- Being **G**ood
- Showing **G**oodness
- Feeling **G**reat
- Showing **G**reatness

While 2G is about how we feel at a basic level and manifesting that with others (remember, we are talking of "showing," not "showing off"), 3G is about getting started on a higher level of feeling for ourselves, and 4G is about manifesting our higher selves and truly surrendering to nature and the cosmos.

It may be worth reemphasizing that, in a media-driven world that drives people to *look* good, it is all the more important for people to *be* good and *feel* good. The rest will happen!

24. Number portability.

It is amazing that we can keep the same number even if we choose to move to a different service provider.

I know of instances where two lovers moved their relationship to a different level. They may not be lovers anymore, but they have a deep sense of respect for each other.

I also know of people who got past one relationship of love and into another relationship of love with the same intensity and feeling and maybe much more. And some who could, but chose not to.

It took me some time to come to grips with this.

I am increasingly realizing that in life we are all actors, meeting and interacting with each other. A better term that I like to use is "life coach."

The act may change, the play may be over, but one cannot take away from having grown a little richer through an experience with a life coach. Didn't Shakespeare talk about all the world's being a stage?

At another level, it also matters as to what one wants to do with the experiences that came with the life coach.

Notes:

Notes:

_____

_____

_____

_____

_____

_____

_____

_____

_____

_____

_____

_____

_____

_____

_____

_____

_____

_____

_____

_____

_____

_____

_____

_____

A log book from Life's Call Center,
where people call in with life questions

"How do I do create a better frame of mind?"

Our frames of mind are shaped by our thoughts.

What is a thought?

It is a word. Read a book that you love!

It is a picture. See something nice!

It is your mood. (Note: it is your mood, not you). Do things you love to do. Be with people who make you feel good, including yourself. (I was tempted to say "Be with people who make you feel happy," but I guess it is only I who can give happiness to myself—unless I have another soul with whom I am "one.")

"How do I learn to be humble?"

We live in a world that still respects humility as a very important DNA.

It takes some effort to realize it.

When was the last time you bent down to touch an elderly person's feet?

You could say, "I don't meet too many elders these days."

Great!

Try this: It might just work. It works for me.

Every night when I lock the door, I bend down to close the lower latch with my hand, rather than my foot. (I closed it with my foot for a long, long time).

If we can bend down for something nonliving (but part of life), I am sure we can bend down for the living.

As they say, the tree with most laden fruit is the one that bends.

Humility begins not with a change but a quick flip of attitude.

Try closing the lower latch of your door with your hand for three months, and you might just realize this.

Can we really learn to be humble? Or can we just "be" humble?

"Where do I find all the answers to my life?"

Life is in some ways measured by the many answers we seek, some of which we are lucky to find.

Life is also measured by the questions we ask and the strength to live with those questions.

The answers show me life for what it is.

The questions show me life for what it is not.

This is because that is not.

That is because this is not.

"How do I turn my sorrow into joy?"

Stand in front of a mirror.

Hold a pen in your right hand.

What do you see? You are holding the pen in your left hand, right?

You see an inverse image.

Imagine now that you were holding sorrow in your right hand.

What would you see now that you have let the mirror in you reflect?

That you are holding sorrow in your left hand or that you are holding joy in your left hand?

If depends on how badly you want to see what you want to see.

Let the rays of life fall onto your mirror, and let life show us the way.

"Does it pay to be emotional in life?"

The undisputed answer to this question is a big "yes!"

Emotions let us express. We express through emotions.

They help us truly manifest.

They help us learn the best.

When was the last time you heard someone feeling sorry because he or she had an intellectual outburst, not emotional outburst?

Emotions are not a trading platform in life. They never can be.

They are as important to us as our bodies, minds, and spirits.

And if we give a little more to our bodies, a little more to our minds, a little more to our spirits, and a little more to our emotions, they will give it all back—a lot more of our bodies, a lot more of our minds, a lot more of our spirits, and a lot more of our emotions.

It is also a fact that the best-performing businesses are very emotional organizations. Maybe we could take a cue from that.

"How much of attachment do I show? Isn't it best to be detached?"

When we drive our cars in the morning, do we plan to what extent we will be attached to the car that morning, or would we rather believe that we will do it together?

It doesn't matter what the roads are.

It doesn't matter whether it will or will not rain.

Life is a lot like that. We do the attachment and detachment together.

We are attached enough to feel, to connect.

We are detached enough to observe, to view.

If we attach too much, don't be surprised, if the car stops working, we end up sitting on top of it, ordering it to move when all it needed was a slight push!

"How did my parents stay married for that long? What's the formula?"

Maybe the formula for a long marriage has to do with two key cornerstones.

One is the extent of emotional attunement. A friend of mine made me conscious of this when he asked, "How many times have you seen your mom ask your dad whether he needed a cup of tea, as if she knew he was on the threshold of a headache?"

It comes with complete surrender to each other.

The other is the realization that the mom that dad they knew ten years ago have also changed as people. Both of them have flown through life like a river, never being the same every moment.

To that extent, it is never monotony but variety that they bring to each other.

Don't they say that variety is the spice of life?

"How can I be a perfect human being?"

I'm not sure if there is anyone one could call a perfect human being. On the other hand, every human being is perfect. Life consciousness is needed in order to manifest this perfection.

Swami Vivekananda once said, "Education is the manifestation of perfection already in man."

He also talked of religion and other life pillars in the reference frames of manifestation and perfection.

Maybe there is merit in starting by being a perfectionist as much as possible. For example, how about knowing what you carry in your wallet and tidying up the wallet to start with?

When was the last time you signed a credit card slip at ease and perfectly, rather than scribbling something in a hurry? I have seen this; people who take the time to sign their signatures well are also people who live life passionately. Think about this: if we don't even have the time to validate our identity with a signature peacefully, when will we ever make the time to validate ourselves in life?

Start with taking your signature seriously. It might help!

"How do I control my anger?"

Until recently, I admit that I had my challenges with anger to the extent that, even when I was not angry and was trying to share something passionately and reflecting on some sad moments with someone, I was misunderstood as being angry.

At least that's what I thought.

There are two aspects to anger.

One is to understand the basis of the anger.

The other is to do something about it.

There are coaches and clubs that teach people 101 ways to manage their anger. I wonder if there is also a book called "Anger Management for Dummies"?

They key to anger management, from what I have experienced, is to understand the basis for anger.

Most often we are angry because we are not comfortable or we are sad with a situation and do not find someone with whom we can share this openly.

Many times I did not share a sad part of me with someone close because I thought I did not want to inundate that person with sad thoughts, and in the process I made it worse. I inflicted my anger on that person for something that had nothing to do with the person, but only with me. Unfortunately, these can never be collateral damages. These are damages in life (not "for" life because effort and faith can change it all.)

That is a realization. I was in a situation today where I might have blown my top if this had been a year ago. I am proud to say I didn't let anger manage—or, rather, mismanage—me.

At a tactical level, I started wearing an anger management band. Every time I felt like I was becoming angry, I held the band, and that would make me conscious and calm me down. As if by providence, one day I was filling a glass with water and the band snapped, as it got entangled with the tap. Today I wear an imaginary band in the same place, and for every day I don't end up being angry, I kiss that band before I go to sleep.

My record in the past three months has been just one day of anger.

I commit to go 365 days back to back this year. I know I can do it! That's the most conscious I ever got about something that has taken me no effort to erase some of my most seemingly painful (but Life enriching) moments with people close to me.

"What is faith?"

Faith is running into a battlefield to rescue your loved one, even if you have never fought a battle.

Faith is what the mother showed by lifting a car when her baby was under it. (This is a true incident!)

Faith is living one's life inspired by that one person one loves the most and doing everything it takes to share that love (in a pure way) with people who need it, without any expectations, even if it means not marrying for a lifetime, and staying committed in body, mind, and soul.

Faith is the chicken that was meant to die but that spreads pleasure even after death through that sandwich and burger.

Faith is being okay with the rain, knowing full well that the rainbow will follow.

Faith is what it takes to move mountains.

Faith moves nations. Faith moves people.

Faith got me my medicine when I ran out of money. I always knew there was this tablet somewhere out there, and lo, there it was.

Faith is getting me through my entrepreneurial journey.

Faith is also taking me through life.

Faith is not so much about what the future holds as it is about what's inside me to make that future happen, bit by bit, starting today, starting now.

Faith is something that shows up suddenly in the toughest situations of life, just like that. At the flip of a moment, faith emerges. It reminds me of quantum physics, where faith lets a particle "leap" from here to there at the same time. No wonder they call it "the leap of faith."

Faith is like the popular game that gives you unlimited chances to succeed, irrespective of how many times you fail, as long as you don't quit the game.

Faith doesn't let one quit the game. It not only keeps one in the game (of life), but also at it.

FAITH is Fully Awakened (to) Inside Thy Heaven.

Faith will show me the door, and life's gates will open.

"How do I start respecting people?"

I am learning that the best way to do this is to start with those who maybe underprivileged . . .

When will you stop cursing the beggar who came knocking on your car window at the traffic signal? When was the last time you offered tea to your domestic help and even made it the way he or she likes it?

Did you ever take you shawl off on a cold, wintry morning when you were out for a walk and wrap it around the old man sitting in a corner, shivering to death? (Shivering to death does happen in many cities worldwide)

When was the last time you made your sick driver sit behind while you chauffeured him around?

When was the last time you paid for the old lady standing in the queue behind you at the tube station?

When was the last time you touched your parent's feet?

When was the last time you looked at your lover, not as a person of desire but as a human being who needs respect and all that comes with it?

(Do take this seriously: as love makes it, lack of respect may break it!)

"How can I find the simple pleasures of life in my everyday life?"

Try these practices:

- Apply your toothpaste completely over your toothbrush, covering all the bristles. Start your day 100 percent loaded!
- Don't read the newspaper first thing. Hold it until lunch. At best, a quick scan of headlines postbreakfast should do. Start your day with a life book or maybe a comic—something nice and warm.
- If you are one of those who love reading horoscopes, try what I did and stay away. If that is tough, read them before you go to sleep and reflecting on whether what it said truly reflected the highlights of your day. You will find the answer for yourself. I have nothing against horoscopes and the "science" behind it, but let it be a point of reflection for you and not necessarily a few lines that control your day from the morning. I reiterate that what is on your hands is also in your hands.
- When you're having breakfast, don't do anything else. Just have breakfast. Enjoy the feeling of what you are eating. Contemplate and thank in your heart all the people who have brought the food to your table.
- While driving to work, listen to something motivating. If you don't drive to work but work from home, you can still listen.
- Chat with all your goodness the people you meet every day: your domestic help, the person who comes to collect your garbage, your laundry person, your newspaper-delivery

person, the person who comes to clean your car, and all the rest.

- Access your mobile phone's messages and mail only after you have spent some time with yourself. If you wake up at 6 a.m., get to your mobile phone only after 8 a.m. We all need time to get ready to interface and interact with all.

- Surprise one person positively! It doesn't matter who. Bring a smile to that person's face. It could be a bouquet that you send to your aged parents. It could be dropping in at a friend's place. It could be picking up and calling someone you have not spoken to for ages. It could be making dinner for your family. It could be surprising yourself with a new hairdo. Just do it!

- Write "thank you" on a Post-It and paste one every day on someone's desk, on your son's lunchbox for something that happened for which you were truly thankful but couldn't say it. If you don't find a reason to thank anyone that day, just put it up on your dressing table mirror or your computer to thank yourself for the very thought of wanting to thank someone else that day!

- Hug your near-and-dear ones every day. A hug may be one of the most divine of human expressions and could say much more than a picture or a thousand words. I would travel the seven oceans for a nice, warm hug.

- Make sure you have one meal with the family, sitting together at the dining table. I am assuming you are blessed to have a family. If you are single, try having a meal at the dining table. Pull up an extra chair and leave a clean plate on the table, waiting for your loved one to come and have a meal with you some day. For now, believe that God will continue to provide you company.

- Wear clean, pressed clothes, even when you are at home. It will make you feel nice!

- Continue to provide positive affirmations. I make use of the mirror above my car's dashboard to tell positive things to myself. Smile. Look yourself in the eye. It is like a little friend tucked away in the car.

- Why celebrate Fridays and weekends only? Celebrate Mondays too. Tell yourself, "Thank God it's Monday!" Look at the immense possibilities for things you could do throughout the week and put the seconds into the minutes.

- Wrap up your day with a little prayer before you sleep. You can let your favorite Teddy bear join you while you pray. In fact, you can hold Teddy and pray together. If you can involve a nonliving person while you are praying, you can certainly involve living beings better. For that moment, for the next day, and for life.

Notes:

_____

_____

_____

_____

_____

_____

_____

_____

_____

_____

_____

_____

_____

_____

_____

_____

_____

_____

_____

_____

_____

_____

_____

Notes:

_____

_____

_____

_____

_____

_____

_____

_____

_____

_____

_____

_____

_____

_____

_____

_____

_____

_____

_____

_____

_____

_____

_____

_____

Notes:

_____

_____

_____

_____

_____

_____

_____

_____

_____

_____

_____

_____

_____

_____

_____

_____

_____

_____

_____

_____

_____

_____

_____

Notes:

_____

_____

_____

_____

_____

_____

_____

_____

_____

_____

_____

_____

_____

_____

_____

_____

_____

_____

_____

_____

_____

_____

_____

An Ode

Floating in life,

Where will I not go.

Perhaps someday I will meet you at the other end of the
  archipelago.

Floating in life,

Why do I so feel the rain?

Was it pouring to wash away the pain?

Floating in life,

Perhaps you will get to be

The feeling of being away and yet being me.

Floating in life,

As the moon sets, and the sun rises,

People who came and those who left with their advice.

And we thought that fighting the wave

Was brave.

Until I meet you, inside me now,

There will come a day in this new beautiful world and how.

I saw you the first time get off a bird.

I saw you the last time, crowded like a herd.

It does matter what you feel

Because that will be life's keel.

I will draw on what I have of you inside,

I will move ahead, and wish you were beside.

Floating in life,

Where will I not go?

If we were to start it all afresh,

Why can't we live it all in life's crèche?
If coming back to each other would be life's goal,
I wonder in what way, in what role.
The waft of the sunlight
Makes life so bright.
Floating in life,
Where will I not go?
Being far, far away, as far as life could ever take,
If that's what makes it steady, if that's what it takes not to break.
The feeling of coming back, like a log adrift,
Who cares for a compass, when you can make it all shift?
Floating in life,
Where will I not go?
That hotel in ice?
That always looked nice.
That trip to the beach?
If only we could now reach.
That cruise on the yacht,
Far away, from misery and wrought?
In that land of mystery, perhaps, lies a dream.
In this land of life, perhaps, lies some cream.
To churn it all out and taste what it is,
To burn it all over, and live what it is.
Floating in life,
Where will I not go?
The last of my breath will hold it all together,
Perhaps someday, somewhere, never maybe or whether?
Come rain, come sun, come any weather,

Life's touch through you, and the feel of a feather . . . .
Floating in life,
Where will I not go?
I don't know when I will be buried,
I do know what it feels to be dead
And alive yet again,
Having washed away the pain,
As if there were ever a last train,
As if there were ever a rice's grain,
As if the birds on the tree could fly and mutter,
As if happiness were what made them flutter.
The green is in front
And the wall behind.
The sky is so open,
And it's all in the mind.
Maybe we could let the sorrow rest with love in our hearts.
Maybe we could resolve for a fresh, new start?
Floating in life,
Where will I not go?
I wait for that knock on the door.
I wait for that step on the floor.
I wait for that hand on the shore.
I wait for those coffee mugs, that brewing, and a bit more.
That face in the crowd
In a city so loud—
Never was it about ego
Or being proud.
That flight across the seven seas,

That search for inner peace,
That drive to the shrine,
The holy feeling, yours and mine,
The thrill of the wild,
The niceness of being mild,
Of being us, being the joyful child.
Floating in life,
Where will I not go?
If faith could move a mountain,
And a paper could be complete with a pen,
If the fire that lights, is also the one that ignites,
If the man who cares is also the one who fights,
Life is lived by the life that is,
Not by the life that was and those that will be in the coming
    centuries.
If all that it takes is to flip the pancake,
If all that it takes is to let the cake bake,
If all that it takes is a true letting go,
If all that it takes is a true "I don't know."
Life is so rife,
Can it ever be without strife?
The very hands that hurt are the hands that give,
It is the heart and soul within that lets us truly live.
If that is pure,
And we are so sure.
Floating in life,
Where will I not go?
If we can be in the zorb,

Why can't we take life's orb?
If we can go to the highest road,
Why can't we be light like the toad?
If life can be an infinity pool,
Why can't we see beyond it all, and let life rule?
Floating in life,
Where will I not go?
A climb up the tree
That set us free,
A hop onto a cycle
That let us ride,
The look in our eyes
That we could not hide.
Behind the veil of pain
Lies something deep within,
Beyond that look
Lies a lovely brook.
As we wake up to the bird in the tree,
I wonder if this will again set us free?
Another moment, another life's pause—
I wish it were your man on the horse
To hold it all together
Like a bunch of roses.
To weave it together,
A door opens, and another closes.
I hear the crickets tonight in the wild.
God, wake us up, give us back the Child.
There is a circle at the end of the road

That lets us take a turn and leap like a toad.

Floating in life,

Where will I not go?

God give me the strength and show me the way, to continue to love
and hope for You inside me,

More than yesterday and today, and less than the tomorrow that
will be.

Floating in life,

Where will I not go?

FACT IS FICTION LIVED.
FICTION IS FACT NOT LIVED.

www.ingramcontent.com/pod-product-compliance
Lightning Source LLC
Chambersburg PA
CBHW032027290526
45786CB00011B/863